Beyond the Written Word

Exploring Faith Through Christian Art

Eileen M. Daily, PhD

saint mary's press

The publishing team included Christine Schmertz Navarro, development editor; Lorraine Kilmartin, reviewer; Mary Koehler, permissions editor; Penelope Bonnar, copy editor; Andrew Palmer, typesetter and designer; Genevieve Nagel, art researcher; manufacturing coordinated by the production services department of Saint Mary's Press.

Printed in the United States of America

1330

ISBN 978-0-88489-849-8

Library of Congress Cataloging-in-Publication Data

Daily, Eileen M.

Beyond the written word : exploring faith through Christian art / Eileen M. Daily.

p. cm.

Includes index.

ISBN 978-0-88489-849-8 (pbk.)

1. Jesus Christ—Biography. 2. Jesus Christ—Art. I. Title.

BT303.D15 2005

246—dc22

2004024115

Contents

Introduction

Christian Art

In the centuries since the life of Jesus Christ, many people have written about the significance of his life, death, and Resurrection through poetry, songs, scholarly books, and textbooks. But written words are not the only way people have expressed what Jesus Christ has meant to them. For the past seventeen hundred years, people have been creating works of art—paintings, sculptures, stained-glass windows, tapestries, church buildings, movies, and other creations—that communicate the personal significance Jesus's life, death, and Resurrection has had in their lives.

You have likely encountered many words in your experience of religious faith; you have probably read or prayed words or listened to words as they are read or spoken to you. This book gives you the opportunity to put words aside and learn another language of faith—art.

The artworks in this book are all Christian images, primarily from European and North American artists, although several artists from around the world are also represented. Just as Northern European artists have painted Jesus with blond hair and blue eyes, you will notice that African artists have painted him with curly dark hair and brown skin. Though the artwork in this book cannot reflect all Christian cultures, the international artwork holds an important place. The sheer number of Christian pieces from Europe and North America can make it easy for North American viewers to forget that Jesus is present to Christians worldwide. Catholicism is a global faith.

Art in Contrast to Words

Have you ever noticed how words are read? Words are strung together in a line. The reader must read one word, then the next, and then the subsequent words until he or she has read enough words to form a sentence. More words then form another sentence, and so on, until the reader has read a paragraph. Eventually, after some time and many words, the reader grasps some meaning from the author's words.

"Reading" art is different because art is not linear or ordered in the way words are. Ten people appreciating one painting will look at the details in ten different ways. They might all ultimately grasp the same general meaning, but they will probably get there by ten different roads. One person might start by focusing on the people in the painting; another might focus on the landscape; a third, on a small detail in the lower-right corner; a fourth, on the way the artist used light; and a fifth, on the colors. The great thing about appreciating a piece of art is that there is no wrong way to begin. You will also find that the longer you look, the more you see. You will notice facial expressions, postures, colors, emotions, moods, light, interactions, size variations among elements, and so on.

You can use the art in this book on your own, or you can use it in a classroom or a group. If you are working with teachers or leaders, they might use the art in exercises geared toward specific topics. If you are using this book on your own, begin by choosing a painting from the list of paintings, grouped by life topics, in the index on page 31.

Read through the next section, which takes you through a process for viewing a painting. Once you have selected a painting you would like to work with, use the questions on the back cover of this book to understand what the art is communicating.

Viewing a Piece of Art

Let's try looking at a painting. Open this book to the painting *Peter Walks on Water*, on page 17. What do you notice first? The storm? The two figures on the right? The guys on the boat? The color? The light?

Look at the painting a while longer.

Where is your eye drawn? What is the mood of the painting? What can you say about the figures? Which are scared and which confident? Even if you don't know the Bible story this painting depicts, you can begin to figure out what matters in the story just by looking.

Words and art complement each other in Bible stories. In this case, if you read the story of Peter's walking on water to meet Jesus (see Matthew 14:22–33), you might find more meaning in this painting, making the Bible story richer for you. Gradually, you'll notice that the painting has details Matthew leaves out and that it necessarily does not have some details Matthew includes. For example, Matthew doesn't tell us what kind of boat the disciples were in, so the painter made it a boat like those common in his own time and place. Matthew tells us that Peter began to sink, but not how. The artist showed him with one leg sinking and the other still on the surface of the water. What the artist did not include were the words that Jesus spoke to the Apostles and their responses. The best the artist could do was to convey the story through the drama of the painting and the expressions and postures of the people depicted.

Art and Theology or Faith

The point of this book is to help you use art to enhance your study of theology and to contribute to your spiritual growth. Art can do this in several ways. It can make a doctrine or concept more concrete than it would be in words alone. It can spark questions that inspire you to explore or study the story, doctrine, or concept. It can generate curiosity about how the artist's contemporaries understood a concept or story and how that might be different from what you understand today. Christian art can inspire its viewers to be better disciples of Christ and challenge their own behavior. And Christian art can be an opportunity to connect with Christ or the saints in meditation or prayer.

Let's use the same painting from page 17 as an example of how art can contribute to your faith growth. Matthew, the author, points to the power of faith in Christ. Philipp Otto Runge, the artist, makes the point more concretely by showing the doubt and the fear on Peter's face and on the faces of the other disciples in the boat, a picture that contrasts with the firm faith of Jesus as shown by his stance and in his care for Peter. One question this painting might raise is whether fear is the same as doubt, or lack of faith. If that question is significant for you, you might do several things: pursue the question through more books and art; talk to your religion teacher, your priest, or another significant adult; or take note of when you feel fear and ask yourself whether it goes along with a lack of faith. In these ways, you can learn about theology and doctrine through art.

The artist, of our sample painting, painted a boat that looks more like a boat of his own day than one in Jesus's day, and he painted what we see as fear, more than doubt, on the faces of the disciples. These features may make us curious about the context in which the artist painted. What was going on in 1806 in Germany? Until that year, Germany was known as the Holy Roman Empire. In 1806, the emperor dissolved the empire. What we now know as Germany was, in 1806, several German-speaking states with small local governments. Napoleon, in Europe, was conquering territory left and right. When the central government of the German-speaking people was dissolved, is it possible the people feared that their German identity was doomed? They might have expected Napoleon to make them French! Could this be why the artist painted the disciples as fearful? Was he trying to tell the German-speaking people to have faith? Was he communicating that Jesus was there for them—even in their fear? If this kind of thinking interests you, learn more about Germany at this time, or find a biography of Runge to help you work with this or other paintings by this artist.

Yet another way to use art is for your own faith development. Runge's painting asks you to check your own faith-to-fear ratio. Are you like the disciples on the boat who wouldn't even try to walk on water? Are you like Peter, willing to take the risk but not always able to focus your attention on Christ? What can you do to improve your faith-to-fear ratio?

To approach the painting through the lens of prayer, spend some time just looking at the painting. Does a prayer rise up spontaneously? If not, try to notice what you feel while looking at the painting. Do you feel fear? Do you feel a desire to have more faith? If so, ask God for faith. Do you feel gratitude for the strong presence of Christ you see in the painting? If so, give thanks for Christ's presence. Do you notice the greatness of God in the painting? If so, give praise for God's greatness. Any religious painting can be the focus of a meditation on God or on saintliness.

Learning Through Comparing Art

Oftentimes, many questions that arise when studying a painting in depth can be further enhanced by comparing two works of art that share a similar theme or even depict the same biblical story. Notice the similarities and differences between the painting we have been studying so far, *Peter Walks on Water*, and *Calming the Storm*, by Hanna Cheriyan Varghese, on page 14. *Calming the Storm* tells a different Bible story (see Matthew 8:23–27, Mark 4:35–41, Luke 8:22–25) that has some similarities to Matthew's story of Peter in the storm. Ask yourself these types of questions:

- What does Varghese emphasize?
- How does her message about discipleship differ from Runge's?

Anytime you look at multiple paintings of the same story, you get different perspectives on the story. The two versions of the good Samaritan story, on pages 18 and 19, are another opportunity for you to explore a biblical story through comparing and contrasting.

Pope John Paul II on Art

In 1999, Pope John Paul II wrote a public letter to artists. In the letter, he celebrates the rich history between the arts and the Church. The Pope notes that the once strong relationship between art and the Church has grown distant in the past few hundred years. The letter calls for a renewed partnership between the arts and the Church.

The Pope celebrates many positive aspects of art, including these three dimensions:

- Art makes visible and attractive those features of God that are invisible.
- Art nourishes while it teaches.
- Art can be a source of theological thinking.

As you use this book, invite yourself to open up to these aspects of art.

Pope John Paul II invites the artists of the world "to use your creative intuition to enter into the heart of the mystery of the Incarnate God and at the same time into the mystery of man" (No. 14). You may be among the artists to whom the Pope is speaking. If the art in this book inspires you, consider pursuing a creative path as a vocation or a hobby.

Creation of Adam
Michelangelo
Rome, Italy, 1512

In this famous image, painted by Michelangelo on the ceiling of the Sistine Chapel, God passes the spark of life to Adam.

Adam and Eve
Komang Wahyu Sukayasa
Indonesia, 2001

The beauty and richness of God's orderly Creation is emphasized in this painting, yet Eve is reaching for the fruit from the serpent (see Genesis 3:1-24). In what ways do people today still reach for more than what is given to them?

Wise Men from the East
Agha Behzad
Iran, 1958

This painting, from Iran, of the Nativity does not contain images of angels or the star of Bethlehem. Why do some paintings emphasize the human nature of Jesus's birth while other paintings emphasize his divine nature?

Detail of the *Moone Cross*

from a monastery
Ireland, ninth century

This detail of one side of the base of the cross depicts the flight into Egypt (see Matthew 2:13-23) and the five loaves and the two fishes (see Matthew 14:13-21, Mark 6:30-44, Luke 9:10-17, John 6:1-14). These carvings symbolize the destiny of Jesus and his saving actions. What meaningful symbols would you carve at the base of a cross today?

The Wedding at Cana
from the Jesus Mafa Collection
West Africa, late twentieth century

Jesus has his back to us while Mary tells him it is time for him to express his care for the wedding couple by performing the miracle of turning water into wine (see John 2:1–11). Might his back's being turned symbolize his reluctance to make his ministry public?

Calming the Storm
Hanna Cheriyan Varghese
Malaysia, late twentieth century

The artist reflects both the humanity of the Apostles and the divinity of Jesus. Imagine being on that boat.

The Multiplication of Loaves and Fishes
Michael Wolgemut
Germany, 1491

In the miracle of the loaves and fishes, Jesus provides an abundance of food for hungry people. Catholics believe that this miracle is meant to point us to the Eucharist, the nourishment God provides to satisfy our spiritual hunger.

The Woman at the Well
Frank Wesley
India, late twentieth century

Jesus shocked people, perhaps even the woman herself, by talking to her. It was improper to speak with women or Samaritans. What kinds of people do we classify as improper to speak with today? Is there a way we can safely reach out to them?

Peter Walks on Water
Philipp Otto Runge
Germany, 1806

Saint Peter's walking on water is a classic biblical story about having faith in Jesus.

The Good Samaritan

Rudolfo Arellano
Nicaragua, 1981–82

Although the road traveled by the good Samaritan would have been rugged and mountainous, this portrayal sets it in the lush landscape of the Nicaraguan countryside. By illustrating Jesus's stories in settings we are familiar with, artists help the stories come alive for us.

The Good Samaritan (After Delacroix)
Vincent van Gogh
France, 1890

Jesus taught about morality by using parables, such as the parable about the good Samaritan (see Luke 10:25-37), illustrated here by Vincent van Gogh. What is Jesus teaching us about who our neighbor is through the story of the good Samaritan?

The Last Supper

Sadao Watanabe
Japan, 1984

This batik seems to depict that part of the Last Supper when Jesus has just announced that one of the Apostles will betray him (see Matthew 26:17-30, Mark 14:12-26, Luke 22:7-23). What does it take to get you to appear as dark and depressed as some of these disciples appear to be?

Gethsemane: "If it is possible, may this cup be taken from me."
Ni Ketut Ayu Sri Wardani
Indonesia, 2002

This painting of Jesus's moment of prayer at Gethsemane is one of a series. This one focuses on the moment of Jesus's suffering before he expresses his surrender to the will of the Father. What human emotion does the artist portray here? When do you feel that emotion? Can you turn to God?

Christ Crowned with a Crown of Thorns
Albrecht Altdorfer
Austria, 1518

By showing the violence associated with the Passion and death of Jesus, artists remind us how much he suffered for us. Do the depictions of violence in today's popular media have a positive value?

Christ on the Cross
Giovanni Domenico Tiepolo
Venice, Italy, mid-eighteenth century

And being found in human form,
he humbled himself
and became obedient to the point of death—
even death on a cross.
(Philippians 2:8)

Detail from *Mystic Crucifixion*

Sandro Botticelli
Florence, Italy, mid-1490s

In this detail from a larger painting, Mary Magdalene clings to the foot of Jesus's cross. Her presence at the cross when many of the other disciples have already fled is a sign of her courage and devotion to Christ.

The Pilgrims of Emmaus
Henry Ossawa Tanner
United States, 1905

When Jesus appears to two disciples walking to Emmaus in Luke 24:13–35, they do not recognize him. Then when Jesus blesses and breaks the bread for their meal, as depicted in this painting, they suddenly recognize him as the risen Christ. When have you unexpectedly encountered Jesus?

The Descent of the Holy Ghost
Sandro Botticelli
Italy, late fifteenth century

In this painting, Mary and the Apostles are receiving the Holy Spirit at Pentecost. Do you think the artist conveys the importance of Mary? How?

The Holy Spirit
from Saint Peter's Church
Fallbrook, California,
late twentieth century

This stained-glass window from a Catholic church in California shows the Holy Spirit showering gifts upon the world. Notice the use of symbolic numbers: three rays of light, seven tongues of fire. In Church teaching, what is special about these numbers?

The Penitent Saint Peter
Simone Cantarini
Italy, 1640s

Why is it important for all of us, great and small, to be sorry for our sins and the harm we have caused?

The Ladder of Ascent

from the Monastery of Saint Catherine at Mount Sinai Egypt, twelfth century

This icon illustrates the theme of an instruction manual for monks living in the sixth century. The monks struggle to ascend to heaven, but sin pulls them off the path. What pulls you away from the path to God?

The Last Judgment
Italo-Byzantine painting, thirteenth century

This image of the Last Judgment is strongly based on Matthew 25:31–46. Notice those who are saved at Jesus's right hand and those who are damned at Jesus's left hand. See also that Jesus's body is surrounded by an almond shape, which symbolizes his resurrected power and glory.

Index of Art by Subject

If you are looking for material to process a particular issue or event, this index will guide you to a painting that will help you consider the situation in a new way. See the back cover of this book for questions to ask yourself when exploring a piece of art in depth.

Acknowledgments

The scriptural quotations contained herein are from the New Revised Standard Version of the Bible, Catholic Edition. Copyright © 1993 and 1989 by the Division of Christian Education of the National Council of the Churches of Christ in the United States of America. All rights reserved.

The quotation on page 8 is from *Letter of His Holiness Pope John Paul II to Artists* (1999), number 14, at *www.vatican.va/holy_father/john_paul_ii/letters/documents/hf_jp-ii_let_23041999_artists_en.html,* accessed September 22, 2004.

To view copyright terms and conditions for Internet materials cited here, log on to the home pages for the referenced Web sites.

During this book's preparation, all citations, facts, figures, names, addresses, telephone numbers, Internet URLs, and other pieces of information cited within were verified for accuracy. The authors and Saint Mary's Press staff have made every attempt to reference current and valid sources, but we cannot guarantee the content of any source, and we are not responsible for any changes that may have occurred since our verification. If you find an error in, or have a question or concern about, any of the information or sources listed within, please contact Saint Mary's Press.

Art Credits

Page 9: Canali Photobank, Milan/SuperStock
Page 10: Komang Wahyu Sukayasa
Page 11: Courtesy of Stony Point Center, Stony Point, New York
Page 12: CM Dixon
Page 13: Vie de Jésus MAFA, 24 Rue du Maréchal Joffre, F-78000 VERSAILLES; *www.jesusmafa.com.* All rights reserved.
Page 14: Hanna Cheriyan Varghese
Page 15: Archives Charmet/Bridgeman Art Library
Page 16: Frank Wesley, courtesy of Asian Christian Art Association
Page 17: Bridgeman Art Library
Page 18: Rudolfo Arellano, Solentiname, Nicaragua, courtesy of Hermann Schulz and Father Ernesto Cardenal
Page 19: Kröller-Müller Museum, Olterlo, Netherlands/SuperStock
Page 20: Sadao Watanabe, courtesy of Asian Christian Art Association
Page 21: Ni Ketut Ayu Sri Wardani
Pages 22 and 29: Erich Lessing/Art Resource, New York
Page 23: Private Collection/Bridgeman Art Library
Pages 24 and 30: Burstein Collection/CORBIS
Page 25: Réunion des Musées Nationaux/Art Resource, New York
Page 26: Birmingham Museums and Art Gallery/Bridgeman Art Library
Page 27: Gene Plaisted
Page 28: Courtesy of Smith College Museum of Art, Northampton, Massachusetts. Gift of Mr. And Ms. Anthony L. Michel (Sarah Prescott, class of 1930)